Comic-Strip Map Skills

by Michael Gravois
Illustrations by Jim Palmer

S C H O L A S T I C
PROFESSIONAL BOOKS

New York • Toronto • London • Auckland • Sydney
Mexico City • New Delhi • Hong Kong • Buenos Aires

DEDICATION

• •

To my mother, Karen, for helping me navigate the map of life.

— M.G.

To Jo Lynne, who's helped me navigate the bumpy roads and happy trails.

— J.P.

Cover design by James Sarfati
Interior design by Michael Gravois
Interior and cover illustrations by Jim Palmer

ISBN 0-439-21557-9

Printed in the U.S.A.

TABLE OF CONTENTS

INTRODUCTION

About This Book

Humor should be an important part of every school day. A classroom that encourages laughter is one that students will be excited to attend. As a teacher, I try to establish a classroom environment that is fun and challenging, knowing that these are essential ingredients to producing motivated students.

This book embraces that philosophy by using a device that students enjoy—the comic-strip—as a humorous introduction to map-reading concepts. The whimsical tales of the Crittertown creatures explore a variety of skills outlined in the National Geography Standards. Topics include cardinal and intermediate directions, degrees on a compass, reading a map key, reading a map scale (direct and curved distances), using a map grid, parallels of latitude, meridians of longitude, and specialty maps which focus on a variety of themes—time zones, political boundaries, road maps, elevations, populations, economics, weather patterns, floorplans, and historical changes.

Using This Book

The Table of Contents lists the skill related to each of the comic-strips. Topics get progressively more challenging, so look over the questions on the activity sheets to find the skill level appropriate for your class.

As an added extension, each activity sheet includes a "Wrap It Up" problem that encourages your students to further their knowledge—challenging them to create their own maps and charts, to work in small groups or with a partner, or to explore the world around them.

There are a variety of ways these comic-strip activity sheets can be used in your classroom. Here are several suggestions:

• To introduce concepts: Make a transparency of the activity sheet and review it in a whole class setting.

• To encourage cooperative learning: Divide the class into small groups and have them work together to complete the problems.

• To extend knowledge: Students can work individually, solving the problems as work in class or as homework.

• To encourage self-monitoring: Set up a self-paced study unit, allowing your students to complete the activity sheets at their own speed.

• To enhance creativity: Have your students create their own map-related comic-strips, similar to those in this book, which can then be displayed as a humorous bulletin board for all to see.

Name: _____

ALL TURNED AROUND featuring Jackrabbit Jim and Monkey Mike

The face of a compass shows north, east, south, and west, which are called cardinal directions.

1. HERE'S A PUZZLE. WHAT DIRECTION AM I IN RELATION TO THE COMPASS IN PANEL THREE?

ANSWER:_____

2. Find Monkey Mike in the first panel. In what direction is he in relation to the compass in panel three?

_____

3. If Jackrabbit Jim were facing north, what direction would be to his left?

_____

4. If Jackrabbit Jim were facing east, what direction would be to his right?

_____

5. Monkey Mike scurried west to go back to his tree, but remembered that he had forgotten his bananas at Jackrabbit Jim's. He turned around to go get his bananas. What direction was he facing when he turned around?

_____

6. Monkey Mike is facing west and Jackrabbit Jim is on his right. What direction would Monkey Mike have to turn to face Jackrabbit Jim?

_____

7. Jackrabbit Jim is facing south and his home in the briar patch is directly behind him. Which way would Jim have to hop to get home?

_____

8. Here's a tough one. Monkey Mike was facing north. He turned directly around, then turned to his left, and then turned directly around again. Which direction did he end up facing?

_____

WRAP IT UP! In what direction does your desk face?

Name: _____

WHERE THERE'S SMOKE, THERE'S FIRE featuring Fireman Fox and Cowbella

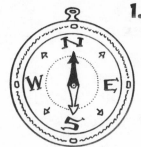

1. **Intermediate directions** fall between cardinal directions. The direction between south and east is "southeast." What is the direction between south and west?

   _____

2. If the firehouse is located southeast of Cowbella's barn, in which direction would Fireman Fox have to travel to put out the fire?

   _____

3. What is the direction between north and east called?

   _____

4. What direction is Fireman Fox in the first panel of the comic strip in relation to the illustration of the compass?

   _____

5. Cowbella was facing southwest as she thanked Fireman Fox for putting out the fire. If Fireman Fox was looking directly at Cowbella, in which direction was he facing?

6. Cowbella ran in a northwest direction out of her barn to escape the fire. When she turned around to look at her barn, in which direction was she facing?

   _____

7. Fireman Fox faced northwest as he sprayed the fire hose into the hayloft. His fire truck was directly to his left. In which direction was his fire truck in relation to where he was standing?

   _____

8. Fireman Fox was facing southeast. What direction was to his right?

   _____

WRAP IT UP! Northeast, northwest, southeast, and southwest are called intermediate directions. What are north, east, south, and west called?

FOOD FOR THOUGHT featuring Topsy-Turtle and Quacker

WHAT'S THE MATTER, QUACKER?

I WENT OUT TO EAT AT A FANCY RESTAURANT WITH SAMANTHA SKUNK AND DORIS DEER.

WELL, THAT SOUNDS LIKE FUN. WHY ARE YOU SO UPSET?

SAMANTHA SKUNK ONLY HAD A SCENT, AND DORIS DEER ONLY HAD ONE BUCK, SO THE COST OF THE MEAL ENDED UP ON MY BILL!

Use the "Food for Thought" map to answer the following questions.

1. After eating at Creature Comforts, Doris Deer went home. She headed north for three traffic circles, southeast for one circle, and then northeast toward her forest. Trace her path with a blue marker. What is the name of her forest?

_____

2. From the restaurant, Samantha Skunk headed southwest to one traffic circle, south to the next circle, and then southwest until she came to the next circle. She lives on the western edge of this circle. Trace her path with a green marker and place a dot where she lives.

3. Fireman Fox left the firehouse to eat lunch at Creature Comforts. In which direction did he have to travel?

_____

4. Quacker decided to leave a visual message for her husband by dropping rose petals along her path. Put red dots along this path. She left the restaurant heading northeast. At the first traffic circle she headed east, then turned southeast at the first circle. At the next circle she headed southwest. After crossing the first bridge she headed northwest. At the third circle she headed northeast to the next circle. She then headed east to the next circle where she turned southeast, back to the restaurant. What was the visual message she left?

_____

5. How many bridges did Quacker cross on her journey?

_____

WRAP IT UP! Write directions for a path on the map. Have a friend trace it.

Name: _____

FOOD FOR THOUGHT: Neighborhood Map

A "traffic circle" is a circular or semi-circular area where several roads come together.

WRONG SIDE OF THE TRACKS featuring Samantha Skunk and Monkey Mike

If you want to be more precise, intermediate directions can be broken down into even smaller increments. North-northeast (NNE) is halfway between north and northeast. East-northeast (ENE) is halfway between east and northeast. The cardinal direction is always mentioned first. Label these two directions on the "Wrong Side of the Tracks" activity sheet.

Use the "Wrong Side of the Tracks" activity sheet to answer the following questions.

1. Monkey Mike ran in the opposite direction of the tiger tracks. Label the abbreviation of this direction on the compass, and draw a picture of Monkey Mike.

2. In which direction is Monkey Mike's tree house? Write the complete direction below and label it on the compass.

_____

3. Topsy-Turtle's log is located halfway between the firehouse and Jackrabbit Jim's. In which direction is it? Write the direction below. Label it on the compass and draw a picture of his log.

_____

4. In which direction is Samantha Skunk's cave?

5. If you wanted to go swimming in Quacker's Pond, in which direction would you have to travel? Write the complete direction below and label it on the compass.

_____

6. Samantha Skunk's schoolhouse is located to the west-southwest. Draw her schoolhouse on the activity sheet and label the abbreviation on the compass.

7. If you completed this page carefully, only one direction has not been written on the compass. Write it below and label it on the compass.

_____

WRAP IT UP! Assume that the seats in your classroom all face north. Create a blank compass, label the cardinal and intermediate directions, and draw icons of one or two objects that are located in each of the directions around you.

Name: _____

WRONG SIDE OF THE TRACKS: Compass Activity

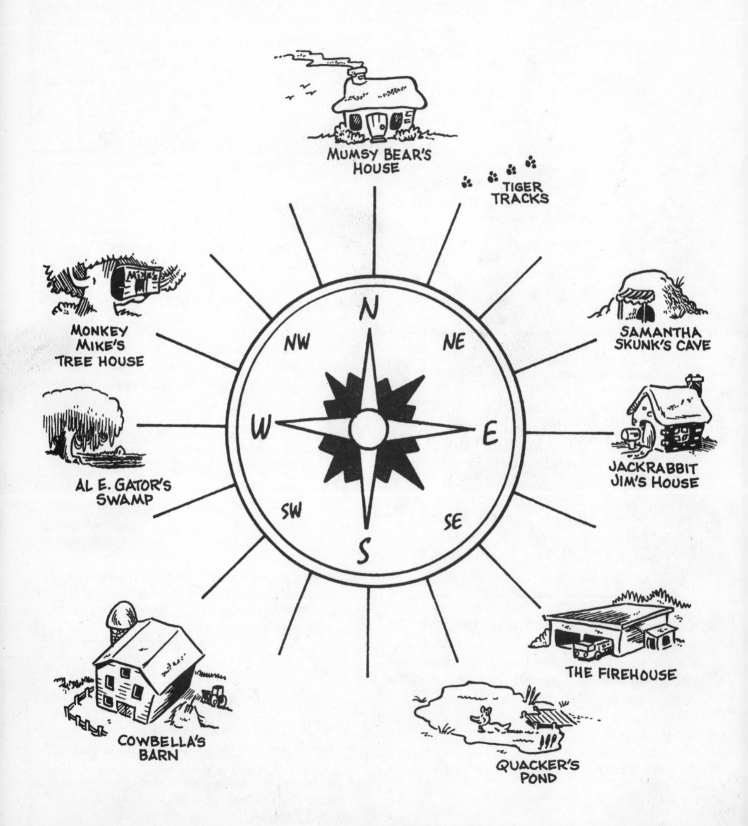

MUMSY BEAR'S HOUSE

TIGER TRACKS

MONKEY MIKE'S TREE HOUSE

SAMANTHA SKUNK'S CAVE

AL E. GATOR'S SWAMP

JACKRABBIT JIM'S HOUSE

COWBELLA'S BARN

THE FIREHOUSE

QUACKER'S POND

IF AT FIRST YOU DON'T SUCCEED featuring Mumsy Bear and Della Dormouse

Use the "If at First You Don't Succeed" activity sheet to solve these problems.

1. Doing puzzle 1 will help you understand how to solve the other problems. Put your pencil on the star. Draw a line three dots north to the square. Put your pencil on the star again. Draw a line three dots southeast to the circle. Put your pencil on the star a third time. Draw a line one dot south-southwest to the triangle. Notice how this line is between the dot that is south of the star and the dot that is southwest of the star. Finally, put your pencil on the circle and draw a line three dots north-northwest to the square.

2. Look at puzzle 2. Put your pencil on the star. Draw a line one dot north-north-east, one dot east, one dot southeast, two dots south, three dots southwest, three dots northwest, two dots north, one dot northeast, one dot east, and one dot south-southeast. What shape did you draw?

3. Look at puzzle 3. Put your pencil on the star. Draw a line one dot west-north-west, one dot west-southwest, one dot north-northeast, two dots northwest, two dots east, one dot north-northeast, one dot south-southeast, two dots east, two dots southwest, and one dot south-southeast. What shape did you draw?

4. Look at dot puzzle 4. Put your pencil on the star. Draw a line one dot north-northeast, four dots east, one dot south-southeast, four dots south, four dots west, four dots north, two dots west, four dots south, and two dots east. Then put your pencil on the circle. Draw a line four dots west and one dot north-northwest. What is the shape that you drew?

WRAP IT UP! Make a dot puzzle of your own, and then write directions for a friend to follow.

Name: _____

IF AT FIRST YOU DON'T SUCCEED: Dot Puzzles

1.

2.

3.

4.

Name: _____

FLYING THE COOP featuring Fireman Fox and Quacker

Compass faces are divided into 360 equal parts, called degrees. East is 90 degrees, south is 180 degrees, west is 270 degrees, and north is 0 or 360 degrees.

1. Quacker is flying north. How many degrees to her right does she have to turn to be flying northeast? (Hint: It's exactly halfway between north and east—0 and 90 degrees.)

_____

2. Fireman Fox is facing north. If he turned directly around to face south, how many degrees would he turn?

_____

3. Quacker is flying southeast. If she turned directly around to fly northwest, how many degrees would she turn?

_____

4. If Fireman Fox wanted to walk southwest, to what degree setting would he have to set his compass?

5. Quacker is standing directly to Fireman Fox's left. How many degrees would Fireman Fox have to turn to face Quacker?

_____

6. Quacker is flying south for the winter. She turns 48 degrees to her left. What would the degree setting on her compass read?

_____

7. Fireman Fox is facing west, and the firehouse is 53 degrees to his right. In order to get to work, what would the degree setting on his compass read?

WRAP IT UP! What degree on the compass is north-northeast? What about west-southwest?

LIVE AND LEARN featuring Mumsy Bear and Baby Bear

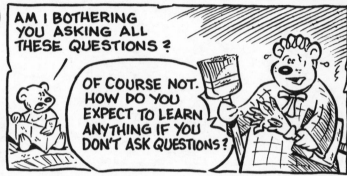

Use the "Live and Learn" activity sheet to answer the following questions.

1. Write the abbreviations for the sixteen cardinal and intermediate directions on the face of the bearing board.

2. Mumsy Bear used a tree that was due north to get the bearing of something that was located in the direction of point A. What is the angle, or bearing, between due north and point A?

_____

3. What is the bearing between due north and point B?

_____

4. What is the bearing between due north and point C?

_____

5. What is the bearing between due north and point D?

_____

6. What is the bearing between point A and point B?

_____

7. Write the letter E on the bearing board for something that would have a bearing of 302°.

8. What is the bearing between north and southeast?

_____

9. Mumsy Bear is facing northwest. How many degrees to her right would she have to turn in order to face point B?

_____

WRAP IT UP! Sextants were used for hundreds of years by early explorers and sailors. Find out what a sextant is and how it benefited these people at sea.

Name:_____

LIVE AND LEARN: Bearing Board Activity

     Before drawing a map, map makers need to measure the exact position of everything to be included. To do this, they set up their equipment at one central point, called a *reference* or *base point*. The land around them is divided up into a series of points, and the distances and angles between the points are measured. The angle between the two points is called the *bearing*, and the people who collect the information are called *surveyors*. For example, the angle or bearing for due east is 90°.

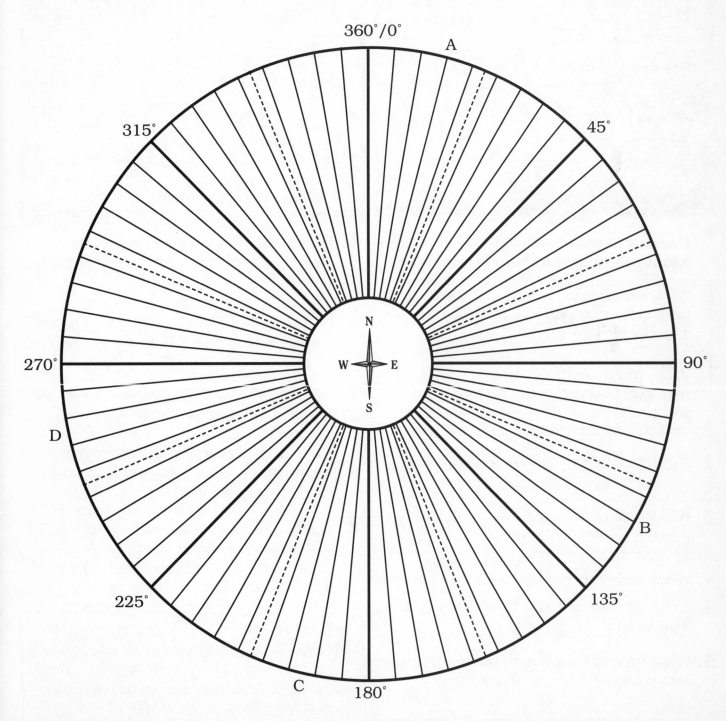

Name: _____

MONKEY BUSINESS featuring Al E. Gator and Monkey Mike

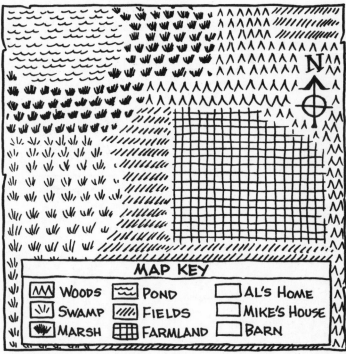

On most maps, a box called a key *or legend* explains all the symbols used. The symbols are usually simple and remind us of the features they represent. A key allows map makers to give plenty of information in a small amount of space.

1. What type of feature can be found in the northwest corner of the map?

_____

2. Color this feature and its corresponding symbol in the key blue.

3. What type of feature forms most of the eastern border of the map?

_____

4. Color this feature and its corresponding symbol in the key green.

5. What type of feature can be found in the south-central section of the map?

_____

6. Select different colors to shade the other four landscape features and their corresponding symbols.

7. Al E. Gator lives in the northeast part of the swamp. Create an icon that represents Al's home and add it to both the key and the map.

8. Monkey Mike's tree house is located in the woods near the southeast corner of the marsh. Create an icon that represents Mike's home and add it to both the key and the map.

9. Cowbella's barn is located in the south-southwest section of the farmland. Create an icon that represents the barn and add it to both the key and the map.

WRAP IT UP! Create and color a map key that includes simple symbols representing the following features: mountains, hills, deserts, plains, beaches, and waterfalls.

Name: _____

CLASS ACT featuring Samantha Skunk and Topsy-Turtle

Use the "Class Act" map and an atlas to answer the following questions.

1. Juneau is the capital of Alaska. Use the key to find the capital symbol. Then add Juneau to the map in the correct location.

2. Barrow is the northernmost city on the map. Use the key to find the city symbol. Then write Barrow on the map in the correct location.

3. What is the name of the northernmost mountain listed on the map?

_____

4. Anchorage is the largest city in Alaska. Draw the appropriate symbol from the key under the first "A" in the city's name.

5. Name the two points of interest located on the map.

_____

_____

6. Label the Arctic Circle on the map.

7. Label the Trans-Alaska Pipeline on the map.

8. The highest mountain in North America is located on the map. What is its name and height?

_____

_____

9. If you were traveling from Anchorage to Fairbanks, in which direction would you need to go?

_____

10. An international border separates Alaska and Canada. In the key, add a dashed line that represents this border.

WRAP IT UP! Draw an outline of your state and create a key that identifies your state capital, major cities, points of interest, and important landforms.

Name:_____

CLASS ACT: Map of Alaska

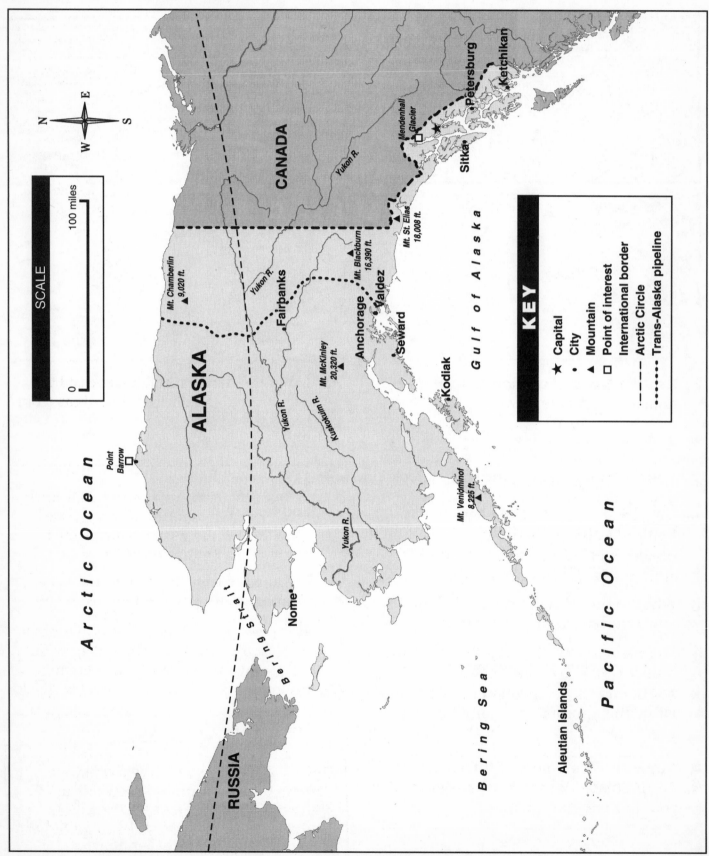

N E
W S

SCALE
100 miles

0

Arctic Ocean

CANADA

Yukon R.

Mendenhall
Glacier

Petersburg

Ketchikan

Sitka

Mt. St. Elias
18,008 ft.

Mt. Chamberlin
9,020 ft.

Yukon R.

Fairbanks

Mt. Blackburn
16,390 ft.

Valdez

Anchorage

Gulf of Alaska

ALASKA

Yukon R.

Kuskokwim R.

Mt. McKinley
20,320 ft.

Seward

Kodiak

Point
Barrow

Mt. Veniaminof
8,225 ft.

Yukon R.

Bering Strait

Nome

RUSSIA

Bering Sea

Aleutian Islands

Pacific Ocean

KEY

★ Capital
• City
▲ Mountain
□ Point of Interest
– – – International border
–––– Arctic Circle
······· Trans-Alaska pipeline

Name: _____

OUT OF SIGHT, OUT OF MIND featuring Jackrabbit Jim and Quacker

1. How far is it from Jackrabbit Jim's house to Quacker's Pond?

_____

2. Jackrabbit Jim and Quacker met each other halfway between their homes before heading to the County Fair. (Put a black dot at the halfway point where they met.) How far did they have to travel from the halfway point to the fair?

_____

3. The next day, Jackrabbit Jim took the bunny trail directly to the County Fair and then returned home. How far did he hop?

_____

4. According to the scale, what distance is equal to one-half inch?

5. How much farther is the County Fair from Jackrabbit Jim's house than from Quacker's Pond?

_____

6. Quacker went to the County Fair and then visited Jackrabbit Jim's house before returning to her pond. How far did she waddle that day?

_____

7. If a map's scale shows that one inch is equal to a distance of two miles, what distance would eleven inches equal?

_____

WRAP IT UP! In which intermediate direction does Jackrabbit Jim live in relation to Quacker's Pond? In which direction does Quacker need to go to get to the County Fair?

Name: _____

MOVING DAY featuring Mumsy Bear and Topsy-Turtle

POPSY BEAR AND I HAVE DECIDED TO MOVE TO ANOTHER STATE.

YOU'VE GOT A GREAT HOUSE. WHY ARE YOU MOVING? IT'S NOT BECAUSE OF THAT PESKY GOLDILOCKS, IS IT?

NO, IT'S BECAUSE POPSY READ IN THE PAPER THAT MOST ACCIDENTS HAPPEN AT HOME.

OH, BROTHER.

= USING A DISTANCE SCALE =

KANSAS CITY • WASHIN
ATLANTA •
• NEW ORLEANS

GULF OF MEXICO

UNITED STATES
SCALE OF MILES
0   100   400   600   800   1000

Use the "Moving Day" map to answer the following questions.

1. Mumsy Bear and Popsy Bear live in Kansas City. They thought about moving to New Orleans, so they drove down to check it out. About how far did they travel?

_____

2. New Orleans was too hot, so they traveled to Boston. About how far is it from New Orleans to Boston?

_____

3. Boston was too cold, so they traveled to Seattle. About how far is it from Boston to Seattle?

_____

4. Seattle was too wet, so they traveled to Phoenix. About how far is it from Seattle to Phoenix?

_____

5. Phoenix was too dry, so they went back to Kansas City, which they realized was just right. About how far is it from Phoenix to Kansas City?

_____

6. How far did Mumsy Bear and Popsy Bear travel on all five legs of their journey combined?

_____

7. How much farther is it from Kansas City to Seattle than from Kansas City to New Orleans?

_____

WRAP IT UP! Would the road distance between two cities be the same as the direct distance on a map? Would it be longer or shorter? Why?

Name:_____

MOVING DAY: Map of the Continental United States

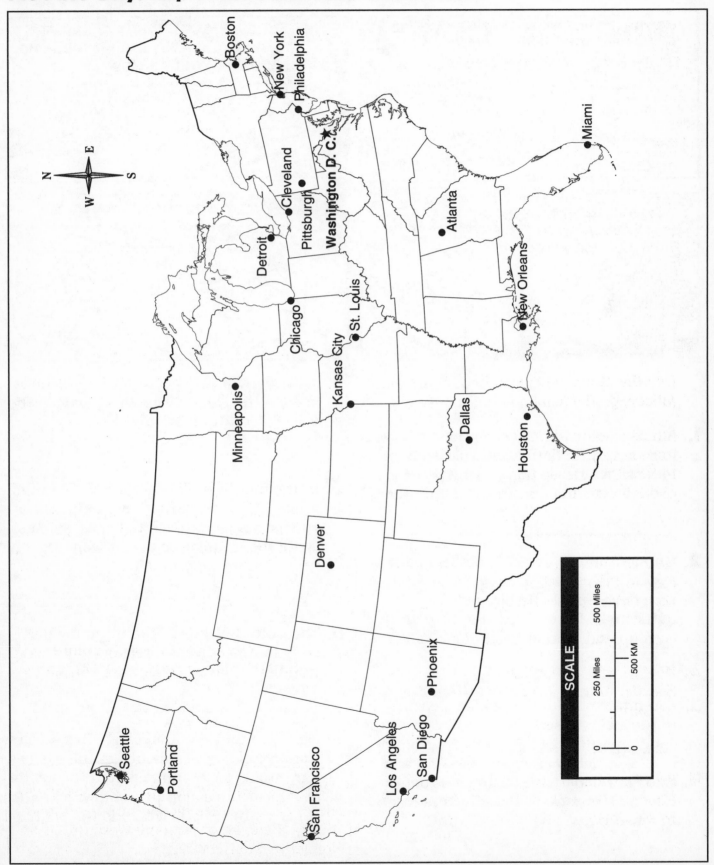

Name: _____

X MARKS THE SPOT featuring Quacker and Al E. Gator

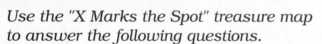

Use the "X Marks the Spot" treasure map to answer the following questions.

1. A clue leading to a treasure chest tells you to go from the edge of Bottomless Pit to Rattlesnake Desert. How many paces is it to go directly from one point to the other?

_____

2. Oh, no! You can't cross Whirlpool Lagoon. Approximately how many paces would it be to go from Bottomless Pit to Rattlesnake Desert by using the path that goes up and around Razor Rock Falls?

_____

3. You find a clue to the hidden treasure in Rattlesnake Desert. It reads, "Start at the gate of pirates bold at the grave from long ago; riches are yours of silver and gold; you don't have far to go. From the gate go 100 paces NW, 125 paces N, and 125 paces NW." Where are you?

4. How many paces would it be to go directly from the gate at Pirates' Graves to the eye of Tarantula Rock?

_____

5. In the mouth of Tarantula Rock you find a note. It reads, "From my mouth count your steps to the desert of rattlesnakes. Write the number below—it won't be long until this mystery breaks."

_____

6. The note continues, "From the tar pit, walk in a northeast direction half this number of paces. Where are you now?"

_____

7. Here you find the final clue: "Draw a line from Skull Island's mouth to the eye of Tarantula Rock; another from the center of Whirlpool Lagoon to a shipwreck, and X Marks the Spot!" Where is the gold?

_____

Name: _____

X MARKS THE SPOT: Treasure Map

Map of Devil's Island
13 November 1542

Name: _____

BIRDS OF A FEATHER featuring Monkey Mike and Jackrabbit Jim

To measure distances along curved roads, you need to use a string. Place the string along the road. Remove the string, marking the distance with your fingers, and then measure the length with a ruler.

1. Monkey Mike went swimming in Quacker's Pond. How far did he have to scamper from his home to get there?

_____

2. After swimming in Quacker's Pond, Monkey Mike went to the General Store to get something to eat. How far did he scamper on this journey?

_____

3. After eating at the General Store, Monkey Mike went home. But then he remembered that he had forgotten to buy some bananas. He returned to the store, bought the bananas, and returned home. How far did he travel?

4. Monkey Mike went jogging one morning. He left home, passed Quacker's Pond, scampered over the footbridge, stopped at the General Store for some MonkeyAde, and then went home. How far was his round-trip jog?

_____

5. How much farther would Monkey Mike have to travel if he went to the footbridge by passing Quacker's Pond than by passing the General Store?

_____

6. If Red, the bluejay, flew directly to Quacker's Pond from Monkey Mike's Forest, how far would she travel?

WRAP IT UP! Draw a map with curved roads. Create a scale. Ask a friend to find the distance between two places on your map.

Name: _____

MEASURE FOR MEASURE featuring Jackrabbit Jim and Wriggle the Snake

Use the "Measure for Measure" map to answer the following questions. Place a string along the curved routes and then measure the length of the string with a ruler.

1. When Wriggle shed his scales, he needed to get a new skin at Jackrabbit Jim's Custom Tailoring. He slithered from his woodpile on Poplar St. and went to Jackrabbit Jim's Shop on Main St. How far did he travel?

_____

2. After work, Jackrabbit Jim left his shop, hopping up Main St. to Park Ave., and on to the boat house in Crittertown Park. How far did he hop?

_____

3. Jackrabbit Jim rented a canoe and paddled from the dock at the boat house to Veronica Lake. How far did he paddle?

4. If you took a train from the Elm St. station to the Pine St. station, how far would the ride be?

_____

5. Topsy-Turtle leaves his pond on First St., turns up Oak St., and attends school on Third St. How far is his trip?

_____

6. Samantha Skunk, who teaches at Crittertown School, catches the train at the Pine St. station. She gets off at Oak St. and walks down to the school on Third St. How far is the trip from the Pine St. station to school?

_____

7. Samantha Skunk invited Quacker to her cave for dinner. Quacker flew directly from her pond to Samantha's cave. How far did she fly?

_____

MEASURE FOR MEASURE: Crittertown Map

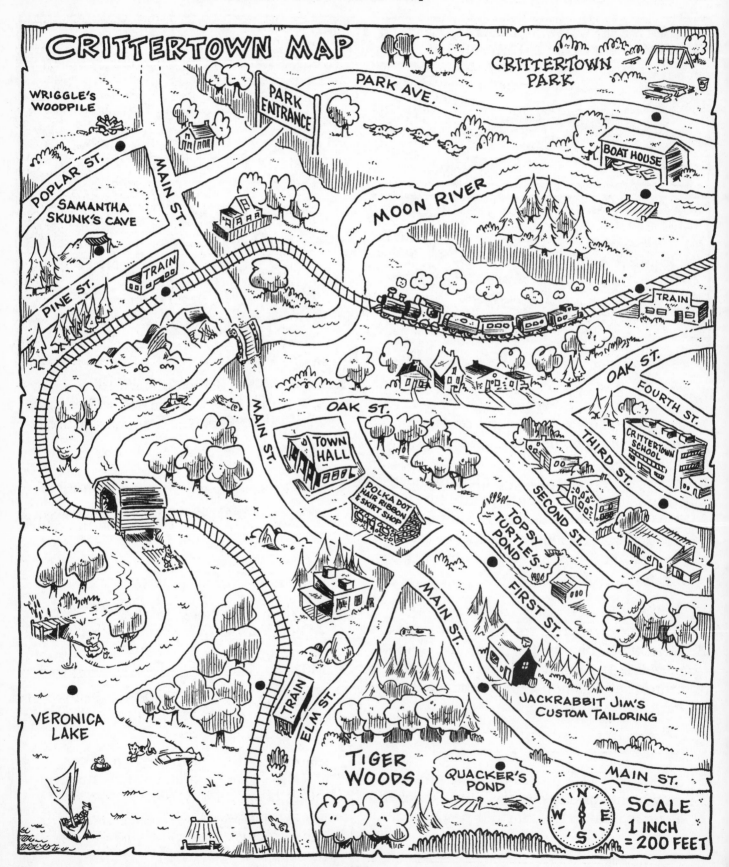

Name: _____

PUZZLED featuring Jackrabbit Jim and Samantha Skunk

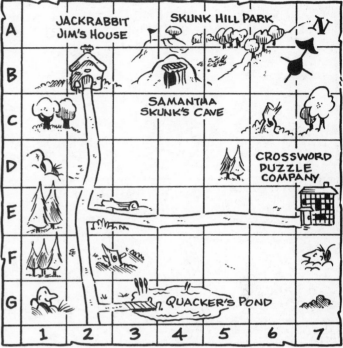

Map grids make it easy for you to locate places on a map. Each square in the above grid has both a letter and number. Find Jackrabbit Jim's house. The letter B is to the left of it, and the number 2 is under it. It is located in square B2.

1. In which square on the grid is the Crossword Puzzle Company located?

_____

2. Jackrabbit Jim followed Samantha Skunk's directions from his house and went three blocks down and five across to get to the puzzle company. Through which seven squares did he travel?

_____

_____

3. In which squares can you find Quacker's Pond?

4. After leaving Jackrabbit Jim's, Samantha Skunk returned to her cave in Skunk Hill Park. In which square is her cave located?

_____

5. In which direction did Samantha Skunk travel to get home?

_____

6. In which direction is the Crossword Puzzle Company from Jackrabbit Jim's?

_____

7. The Palmer Woods are located in squares D3, D4, E4, E5, F5, and F6. Draw them on the map.

WRAP IT UP! Draw a bird's-eye view map of your classroom. Add a grid and create questions for your classmates to answer.

Name: _____

SCHOOL DAZE featuring Samantha Skunk, Baby Bear, and Della Dormouse

Use the "School Daze" map to answer the following questions.

1. In which section of the grid can the state of Massachusetts be found?

_____

2. In which section(s) of the grid can the state in which you live be found?

_____

3. The place where the states of Utah, Colorado, Arizona, and New Mexico all meet is called the Four Corners. In which section of the grid is this located?

_____

4. Parts of which states can be found in square C2?

_____

_____

5. Six states border Nebraska. List each state and the grid locations in which they can be found.

STATE   GRID LOCATION

_____   _____

_____   _____

_____   _____

_____   _____

_____   _____

_____   _____

WRAP IT UP! Draw a map of your state. Include the state capital, major cities, and landforms. Add a grid and create questions for your classmates to answer.

Name: _____

SCHOOL DAZE: Map of the Continental United States

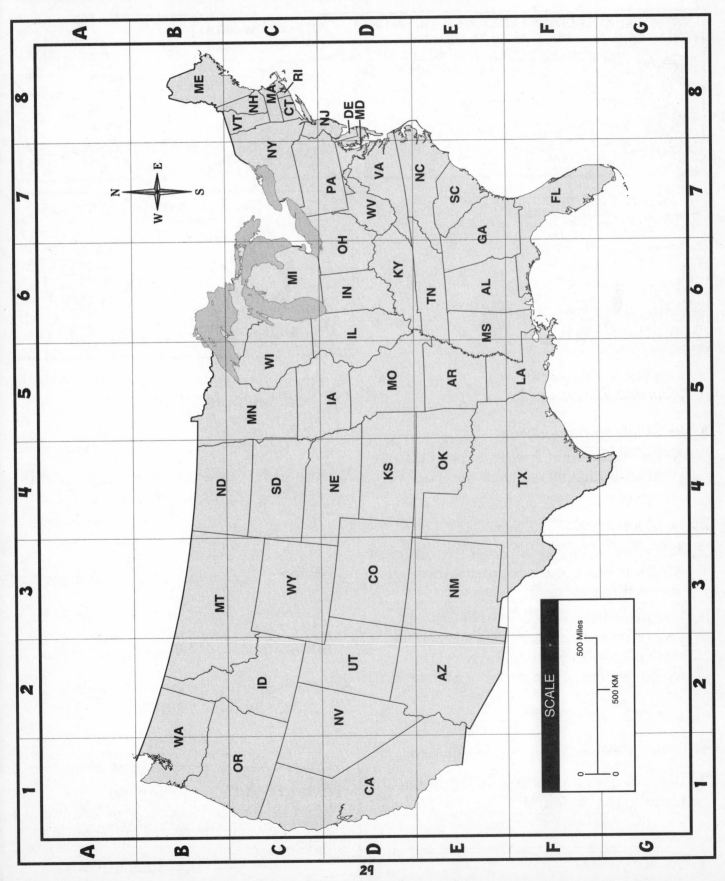

Name: _____

GO CLIMB A TREE featuring Fireman Fox and Al E. Gator

Use the "Go Climb a Tree" map to answer the following questions.

1. The Sahara, the world's largest desert, is in Africa. Approximately which line of latitude passes through its name on the map?

_____

2. The equator passes through the center of Africa. Name the six countries through which it passes.

_____

_____

_____

_____

3. What is the name of the major parallel of latitude that is found at 23 1/2° N?

4. Through which desert does the Tropic of Capricorn pass?

_____

5. At which degree of latitude is each of the following cities found?

Cape Town _____

Cairo _____

Nairobi _____

Khartoum _____

6. Which city on the map is located at a latitude of about 32 1/2° N?

_____

WRAP IT UP! Look on a map of the United States. Which degree of latitude passes through the center of the state in which you live?

Name: _____

GO CLIMB A TREE: Parallels of Latitude

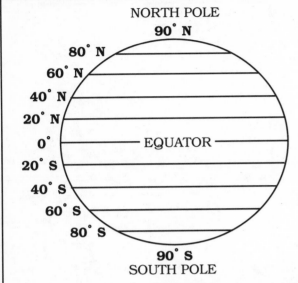

Parallels of latitude are imaginary horizontal lines that run around the earth. The line that runs around the middle of the earth is called the equator. It divides the earth into the northern and southern hemispheres. The other lines of latitudes are north and south of the equator and are parallel to it. Parallel lines run in the same direction and are an equal distance apart at all points. The distance between the lines is measured in degrees. The equator is labeled 0 degrees (0°). The North Pole is 90° N of the equator. The South Pole is 90° S of the equator. All other parallels of latitude fall in between. The line above the equator, on the globe to the left for example, is 20° N. The line below the equator is 20° S.

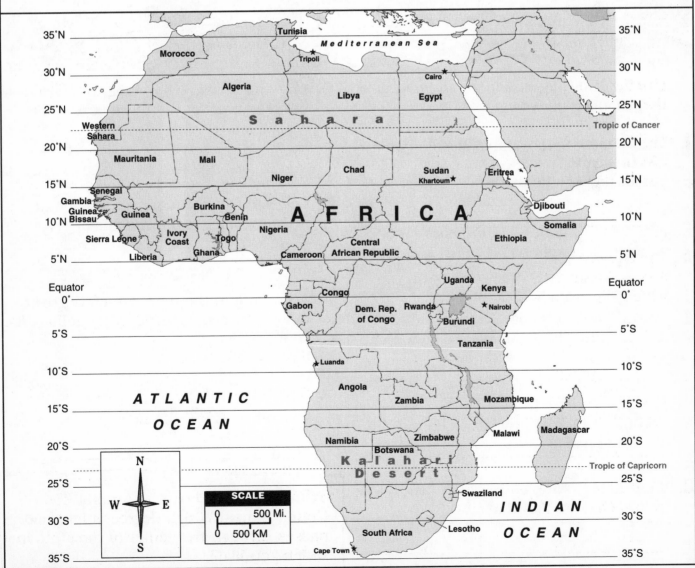

Name: _____

THE SPELLING BEE featuring Samantha Skunk and Baby Bear

Use "The Spelling Bee" map to answer the following questions.

1. Is the Black Sea in the eastern or western hemisphere?

_____

2. Is the city of London in the eastern or western hemisphere?

_____

3. According to this map, estimate the degree of longitude at which London can be found.

_____

4. Through which six countries does 30° E longitude pass?

_____

_____

_____

5. How many degrees of longitude are between each of the meridians shown on the map?

_____

6. The country of Romania can be found between which two meridians of longitude?

_____

7. According to the map, which degree of longitude passes through the following countries?

Italy _____

Iceland _____

Sweden _____

WRAP IT UP! Look at a map of the United States. Which degree of longitude passes through the center of the state in which you live?

THE SPELLING BEE: Meridians of Longitude

Name: _____

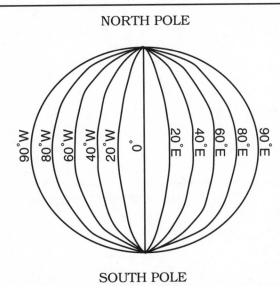

Meridians of longitude are vertical lines that run from the North Pole to the South Pole. They help us measure distance east and west. Meridians are not parallel like the lines of latitude. They are farthest apart at the equator and are closer together at the poles. There are two major meridians of longitude. **The Prime Meridian** runs through Greenwich, England. It is labeled 0° and divides the earth into the eastern and western hemispheres. **The International Date Line** falls on the opposite side of the earth from the Prime Meridian. It is labeled 180°. At the 180° line, east meets west: 180° E and 180° W are the same line.

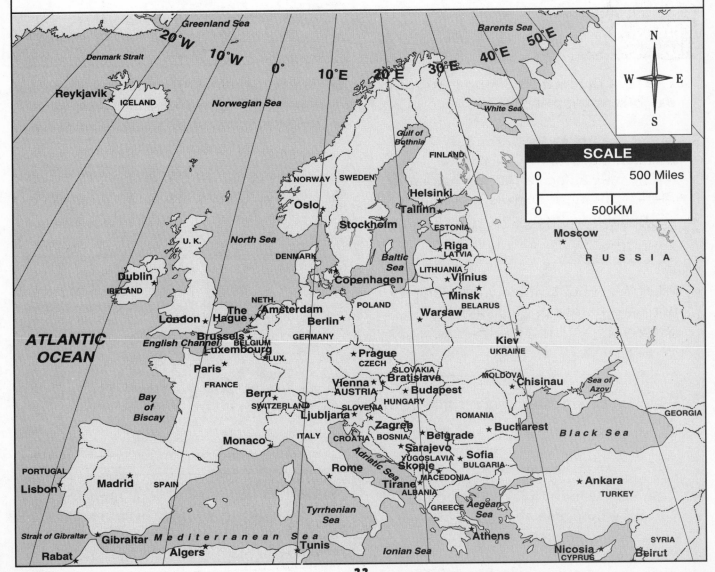

Name: _____

THE DREAM TEAM featuring Quacker and Della Dormouse

Use "The Dream Team" map to answer the following questions.

1. In her dream, Della Dormouse visited Disneyland, which is located in Anaheim, California. At approximately what location, in degrees and minutes, is Anaheim located?

_____

2. What degree of latitude runs along the northern border of California and Nevada?

_____

3. Which state's western border falls near 114° 3'W?

_____

4. Quacker swam in a lake located at 39°N, 120°W. Where was she?

5. At approximately how many degrees longitude is Pyramid Lake located? Use degrees and minutes in your answer.

_____

6. Della visited an island located at 34°N, 120°W. Which island did she visit?

_____

7. Where is Lassen Volcanic National Park located? Approximate your answer using degrees and minutes.

_____

8. What body of water borders southeast California?

_____

WRAP IT UP! Locate your hometown on a map. Write its approximate position in degrees and minutes, latitude and longitude.

Name: _____

THE DREAM TEAM: Map of California

To be more exact when expressing the locations of places, degrees longitude and latitude are broken down into units called minutes. There are sixty minutes between each degree. Minutes are expressed using this symbol (') after the number. For example, if something were located at thirty-seven degrees, nineteen minutes north, it would be written as 37° 19'N.

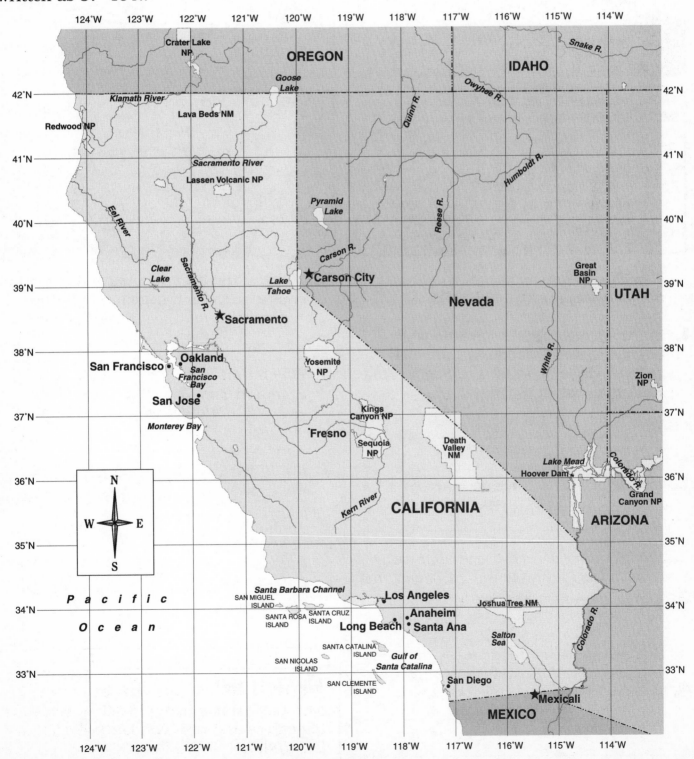

Name: _____

IN THE DOGHOUSE featuring Cowbella and Wriggle the Snake

Use the "In the Doghouse" map to answer the following questions.

1. Cowbella took a trip to Seattle while Wriggle visited Orlando. If Cowbella called Wriggle at 10:00 A.M. Pacific Time, what time was it in Orlando?

_____

2. In which direction are you moving across the country if the time becomes later?

_____

3. In which time zone is it one hour earlier than in the Central Standard Time Zone?

_____

4. How many hours difference is there between New York and Honolulu?

_____

5. Much of the International Date Line runs along which degree of longitude?

_____

6. Which time zone is west of Mountain Standard Time Zone?

_____

7. If it is 1:00 A.M. in Dallas, what time would it be in each of these cities?

Anchorage _____

Chicago _____

Washington, D.C. _____

Helena _____

WRAP IT UP! Why do you think time zones were established? In small groups, brainstorm a list of reasons. Write a paragraph describing your answer.

IN THE DOGHOUSE: Time Zone Map of the United States

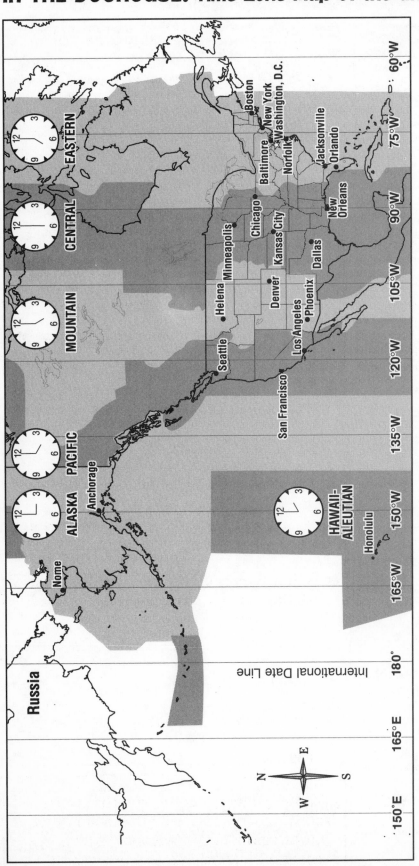

Because of the earth's rotation, some places have daylight while other places have darkness. Each spot on the earth goes from day to night and back again once every twenty-four hours. However, when it is midday at one place on the earth, it will be the middle of the night somewhere else. And at some other spot the sun will be just beginning to rise.

It is important for us to know what time it is all over the world, especially if we travel for business or pleasure or if we make international phone calls. So we have divided the earth into twenty-four time zones, each of which is one-hour wide. The zones are numbered starting at the Greenwich Meridian, which is the zero longitude line. This meridian runs through Greenwich, England. All of the zones west of the Greenwich Meridian are earlier than at Greenwich. The zones east of the Greenwich Meridian are later. Halfway around the world, at 180° longitude, the time is twelve hours earlier than in Greenwich on one side of the longitude line, while on the other it is twelve hours later. This is the International Date Line. If you cross the line westward, you gain a day. If you travel eastward, you lose a day.

Name: _____

THE NAME GAME featuring Topsy-Turtle, Quacker, and Della Dormouse

GOOD AFTERNOON, QUACKER.

HELLO, TOPSY.

WHAT DID DELAWARE TO OUR BASEBALL GAME?

IDAHO. ALASKA.

HEY, DELLA, TOPSY WANTS TO KNOW WHAT YOU WORE TO THE BASEBALL GAME.

WHY, TELL HIM MY NEW JERSEY, OF COURSE.

Some political boundaries can be seen, such as those that lie along coasts, rivers, or lakes. Others are lines that are marked on maps but invisible in the real world, such as those between states or between states and countries.

Use "The Name Game" map to answer the following questions.

1. What three states border New Jersey with visible or invisible boundaries?

_____

2. Name the five visible boundaries of New Jersey that are shown on this map.

_____

_____

3. Which state forms an invisible boundary with New Jersey?

4. What forms most of New Jersey's western boundary?

_____

5. What two state capitals are shown on the map?

_____

6. What four features form the boundaries of Cape May County?

_____

_____

7. How many visible boundaries for Morris County are shown on the map?

_____

WRAP IT UP! How might you know when you are leaving one state and entering another?

Name: _____

THE NAME GAME: Political Map of New Jersey

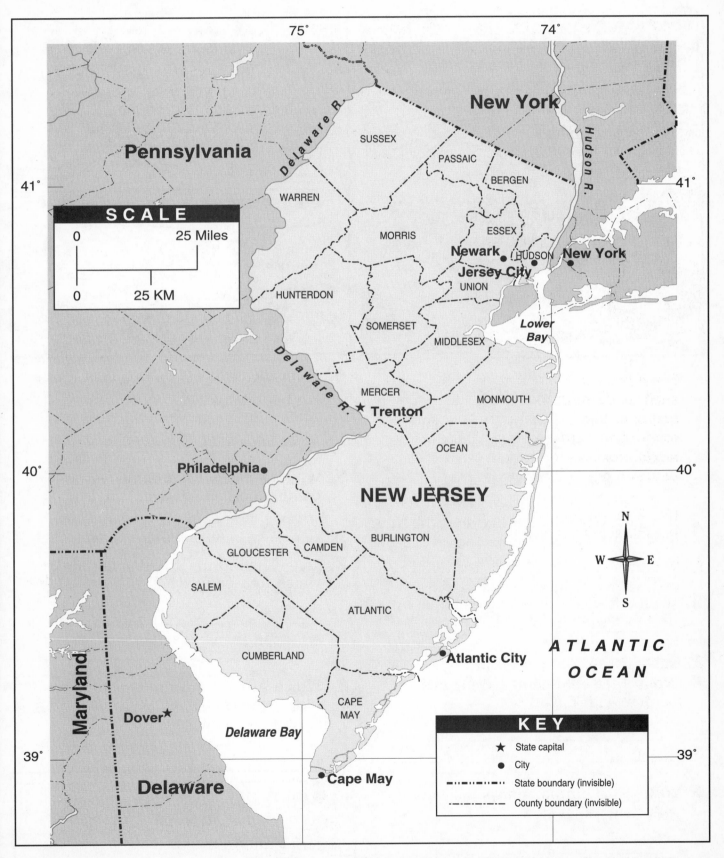

75°   **74°**

New York

Pennsylvania

Delaware R.

Hudson R.

SUSSEX

PASSAIC

BERGEN

41°   **41°**

WARREN

ESSEX

MORRIS

Newark ●   HUDSON   **New York** ●

SCALE

| 0 | 25 Miles |

Jersey City

0   25 KM

HUNTERDON

UNION

Lower Bay

SOMERSET

MIDDLESEX

Delaware R.

MERCER

MONMOUTH

★ **Trenton**

OCEAN

Philadelphia ●

40°   **40°**

NEW JERSEY

BURLINGTON

N

CAMDEN

GLOUCESTER

W ✦ **E**

SALEM

ATLANTIC

S

Maryland

CUMBERLAND

ATLANTIC

Atlantic City ●

OCEAN

CAPE MAY

Dover ★

Delaware Bay

39°   **39°**

KEY

★ State capital

● City

Delaware

Cape May ●

— ··· — State boundary (invisible)

— · — County boundary (invisible)

Name: _____

QUEEN OF THE NILE featuring Cowbella and Fireman Fox

Use the "Queen of the Nile" map to answer the following questions.

1. The Nile River forks into two smaller rivers. What are the names of the smaller rivers?

_____

2. At which city and country does the Nile fork occur?

_____

3. What two visible boundaries make up part of Egypt's borders?

_____

4. What three countries share invisible borders with Egypt?

_____

_____

5. How many countries form invisible borders with Tanzania?

6. Name the three visible borders of Tanzania.

_____

_____

7. Which country is contained entirely within another country?

_____

8. Lake Chad forms a visible border for which four countries?

_____

_____

9. Which African country is actually a large island?

_____

WRAP IT UP! Name the visible and invisible boundaries that form your state's borders.

Name: _____

QUEEN OF THE NILE: Political Map of Africa

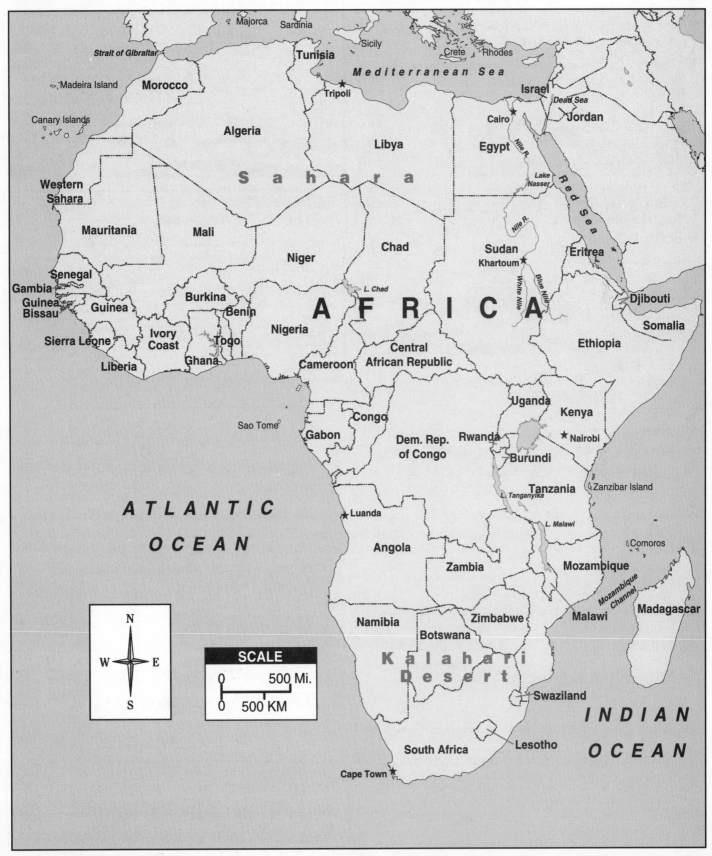

Name: _____

THE ROAD TRIP featuring Mumsy Bear and Baby Bear

Use "The Road Trip" map to answer the following questions.

1. If Mumsy Bear wanted to travel from Phoenix to Flagstaff, what would be the fastest route for her to take?

_____

2. Does Route 191 travel north and south or east and west?

_____

3. Mumsy rode from Utah to California on Interstate 15. In which intermediate direction did she travel?

_____

4. Mumsy traveled from Yuma, Arizona, to Tuscon, Arizona, by interstate. Which two interstates did she use?

_____

5. Routes 666, 264, and 40 all come together at which city?

_____

6. What kind of road is Route 85?

_____

7. Jackrabbit Jim traveled from California to New Mexico along Interstate 40. Through which four cities did he travel?

_____

_____

8. If you take Route 180 north from Flagstaff, where will you end up?

_____

WRAP IT UP! Use a highlighter to trace each of the routes mentioned above.

Name: _____

THE ROAD TRIP: Road Map of Arizona

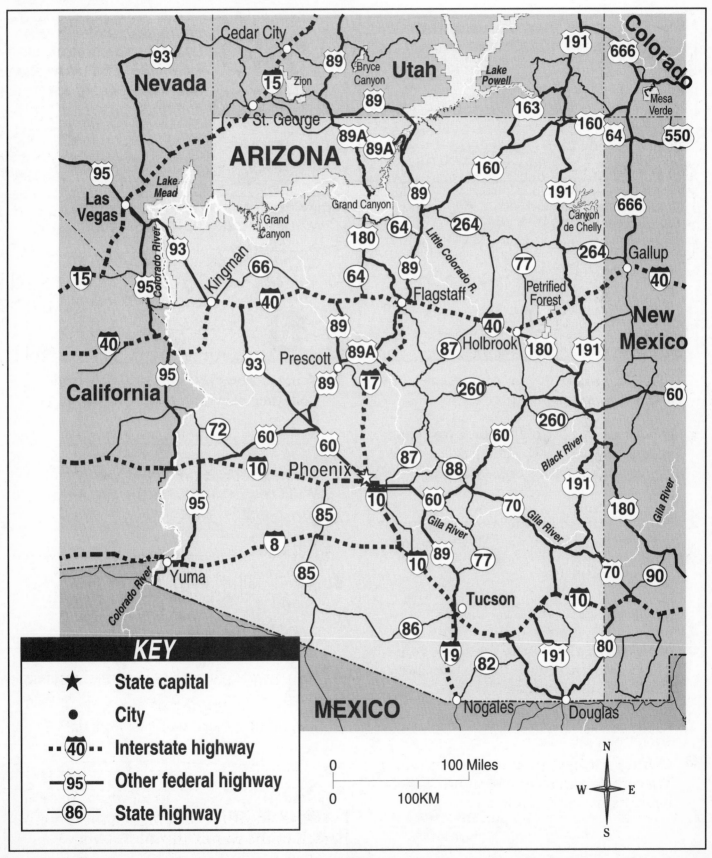

Name: _____

GO FIGURE **featuring Jackrabbit Jim and Cowbella**

THAT MOUNTAIN IS 90,006 YEARS OLD, COWBELLA.

I'M AMAZED! I CAN UNDERSTAND HOW IT MIGHT BE ESTIMATED AT 90,000 YEARS OLD...

...BUT HOW DO YOU ARRIVE AT EXACTLY 90,006 YEARS?

THEY TOLD ME IT WAS 90,000 YEARS OLD WHEN I MOVED HERE SIX YEARS AGO.

Use the "Go Figure" map to answer the following questions.

1. Is Allentown at a higher or lower elevation than Oil City?

_____

2. Which of the following mountain ranges is the highest—Pocono, Allegheny, or Appalachian?

_____

3. What is the highest point in Pennsylvania? What is its height?

_____

4. Which city on the map is located at the lowest elevation?

_____

5. At what elevation is Coudersport?

6. What is the elevation under 0 feet called?

_____

7. In which direction would you travel from Williamsport to reach the highest part of the state?

_____

8. If you walked north from Williamsport would you be going uphill or downhill?

_____

9. Which two bodies of water create visible borders for the state of Pennsylvania?

_____

WRAP IT UP! Find an elevation map of your state. What is the elevation of the city or town in which you live?

GO FIGURE: Elevation Map of Pennsylvania

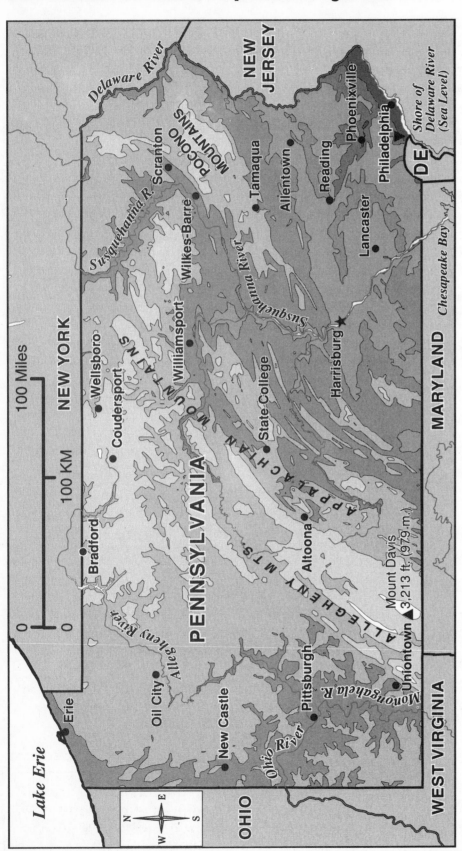

The earth has highlands, such as mountains and plateaus, and lowlands, such as plains and valleys. These three-dimensional features are difficult to show on a two-dimensional map. Elevation maps use contour lines and shading to illustrate the earth's landforms and bodies of water in a two-dimensional picture. To measure the land's elevation, map makers start at sea level, not ground level. Sea level is the height of the ocean where it meets the land along the coast. Using sea level as a starting point allows elevations across the globe to be compared to one another. For instance, Pikes Peak in Colorado is only 7,500 feet above the land around it (ground level), but it is over 14,000 feet above sea level.

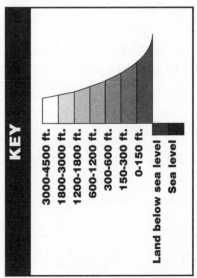

KEY

- 3000-4500 ft.
- 1800-3000 ft.
- 1200-1800 ft.
- 600-1200 ft.
- 300-600 ft.
- 150-300 ft.
- 0-150 ft.
- Land below sea level
- Sea level

Name: _____

THE DOCTOR IS IN featuring Al E. Gator and Mumsy Bear

Use "The Doctor Is In" map to answer the following questions.

1. What is the population in western Ireland? Answer in square miles.

_____

2. Most of which country has over 250 people per square mile?

_____

3. Which region of Europe has the fewest number of people per square mile?

_____

4. How many people per square kilometer live in most of Greece?

_____

5. How many people per square mile live in the central part of Iceland?

_____

6. As you move across Europe from east to west, does the population increase or decrease?

_____

7. List the following cities in order from least crowded (per square mile) to most crowded—Moscow, Athens, Bucharest.

_____

_____

8. Very few people live north of this special line of latitude that runs just above Iceland.

WRAP IT UP! Create a population map that shows the number of people who live in the urban and rural areas of your state.

THE DOCTOR IS IN: Population Map of Europe

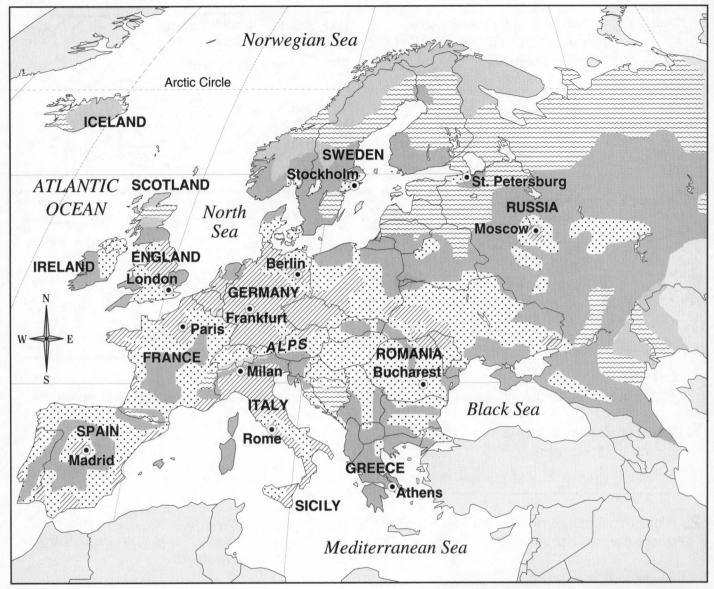

KEY

Per square kilometer	Per square mile
0 to 2	0 to 5
2 to 20	5 to 50
20 to 40	50 to 100
40 to 100	100 to 250
Over 100	Over 250

Population maps use colors, shading, or patterns to show you the number of people who live in a particular area. You can see that the map above uses patterns and shading. What are some of the characteristics of crowded or densely populated areas? Would you expect to find cities in these areas? Are there fewer cities in less-crowded areas? What do you think would be some of the characteristics of places that are less crowded?

DOLLARS AND SENSE featuring Mumsy Bear and Baby Bear

Use the "Dollars and Sense" map to answer the following questions.

1. Which product appears only twice on the map of Montana?

_____

2. Which two products are shown fifteen times each on the map?

_____

3. Name two products that are found near the state's capital.

_____

4. Most of the state's corn is grown in which part of Montana?

_____

5. List the products that are found deep within the earth.

_____

6. According to the map, what animal products contribute to Montana's economy?

_____

7. Which products are grown by farmers?

_____

8. Most of the silver and gold is found in this part of Montana.

_____

9. Which product is often found in the same location as natural gas?

_____

WRAP IT UP! Research the major products that are produced in your state. Create icons that represent each product. The icons should be simple, clear graphics that quickly convey the type of product you're illustrating.

Name: _____

DOLLARS AND SENSE: Economic Map of Montana

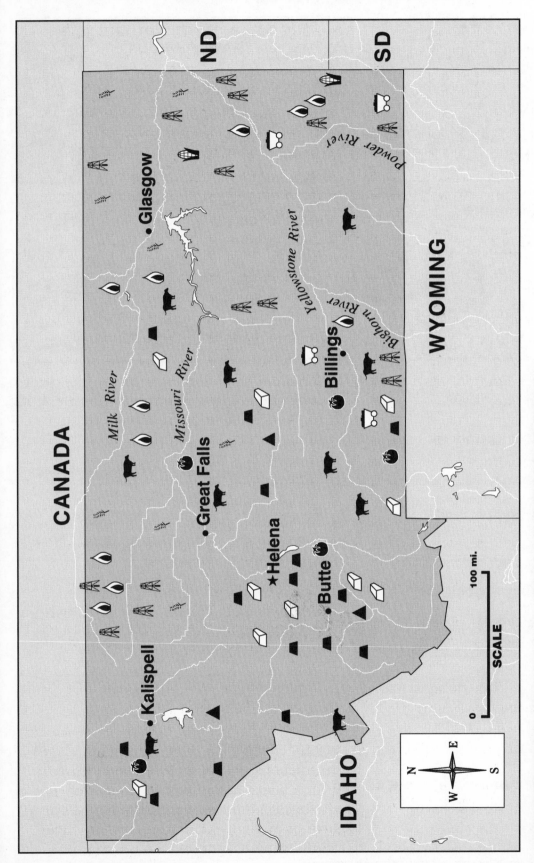

Economic or product maps illustrate the major resources that bolster the economy of a state or country. Some resources are living things, such as plants and animals. Some are nonliving things, such as water, coal, oil, and gold. Others fit into neither category, such as tourism. The map above shows many of the major economic resources of the state of Montana.

KEY

★ State capital   🌽 Corn   ◢ Silver

• City   ◈ Gold   🐂 Cattle

▲ Poultry   ☢ Vegetables   Coal

                     ◈ Natural gas

                     Petroleum (oil)

                     Wheat

Name: _____

FAIR-WEATHER FRIENDS featuring Della Dormouse and Topsy-Turtle

Use the "Fair-Weather Friends" map to answer the following questions.

1. Which city is expecting thunderstorms?

_____

2. Which city is expecting showers?

_____

3. Which city is expecting the coldest weather?

_____

4. How many cities shown on the map are expecting sunny weather?

_____

5. This type of front is sitting along the East Coast.

6. Which of the following cities will experience the greatest fluctuation between its high and low temperatures—Lexington, Albuquerque, or Denver?

_____

7. How many cities are expecting snow?

_____

8. Based on the information provided, which season do you think is shown on the map?

_____

WRAP IT UP! Research your state's all-time record high and low temperatures. Which years saw the most and least precipitation? Find a weather map in your local or national paper, and write questions for your friends to answer.

FAIR-WEATHER FRIENDS: Weather Map of the United States

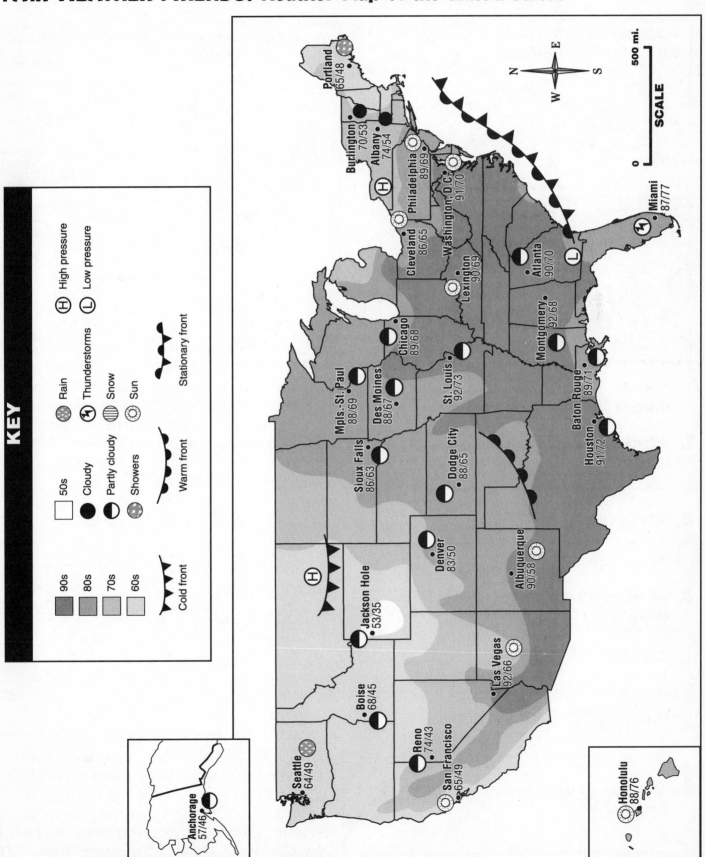

KEY

High pressure Ⓗ	Low pressure Ⓛ	
Rain	Thunderstorms	Snow	Sun
50s	Cloudy ●	Partly cloudy ◑	Showers
90s 80s 70s 60s	Cold front	Warm front	Stationary front

Portland 65/48
Burlington 70/53
Albany 74/54
Philadelphia 89/69
Washington, D.C. 91/70
Cleveland 86/65
Lexington 90/69
Atlanta 90/70
Miami 87/77
Chicago 89/68
Montgomery 92/68
Mpls.-St. Paul 88/69
Des Moines 88/67
St. Louis 92/73
Baton Rouge 89/71
Houston 91/72
Sioux Falls 86/63
Dodge City 88/65
Denver 83/50
Albuquerque 90/58
Jackson Hole 53/35
Las Vegas 92/66
Boise 68/45
Reno 74/43
San Francisco 65/49
Seattle 64/49
Anchorage 57/46
Honolulu 88/76

N E S W — SCALE 500 mi. 0

Name: _____

TAKE A HIKE featuring Monkey Mike and Wriggle the Snake

Use the "Take a Hike" trail map to answer the following questions.

1. Monkey Mike left the Visitor Center and hiked Geyser Pass and Hot Springs Loop. He then returned to the Visitor Center. How far did he hike?

_____

2. Monkey Mike hiked to Vista Bay along Geyser Pass and the Vista Bay Shortcut. Wriggle slithered to Vista Bay along the Rolling Hills Trail. How much farther did Monkey Mike hike than Wriggle?

_____

3. How long is Canyon Ridge Trail?

_____

4. How much shorter is Geyser Pass than Rolling Hills Trail?

_____

5. From the Visitor Center, Monkey Mike went to the Echo Canyon Overlook by going along Geyser Pass to the Echo Canyon Shortcut. Wriggle hiked along Canyon Ridge Trail to the scenic overlook. Who hiked farther?

_____

6. When Monkey Mike became a park ranger he led a tour group along Rolling Hills Trail. Then they took the shortcut over to Hot Springs and returned to the Visitor Center along Geyser Pass. How far did they hike?

_____

7. Which scenic overlook would have a better view of the sunset—the one by Echo Canyon or the one by Vista Bay?

_____

WRAP IT UP! Write a short story about an interesting hike that you once took.

TAKE A HIKE: Crittertown State Park Trail Map

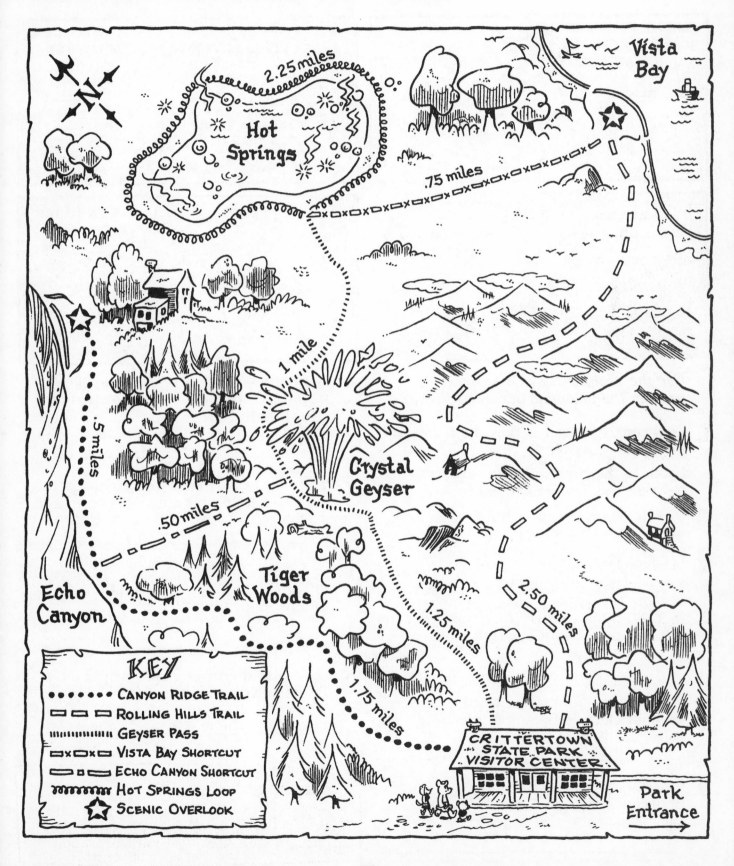

Hot Springs
2.25 miles
.75 miles
Vista Bay
1 mile
.5 miles
Crystal Geyser
.50 miles
Echo Canyon
Tiger Woods
1.25 miles
2.50 miles
1.75 miles

KEY
• • • • • • Canyon Ridge Trail
▭ ▭ ▭ Rolling Hills Trail
▥▥▥▥ Geyser Pass
▭x▭x▭ Vista Bay Shortcut
▭ ▫ ▭ Echo Canyon Shortcut
〰〰〰 Hot Springs Loop
★ Scenic Overlook

CRITTERTOWN STATE PARK VISITOR CENTER

Park Entrance →

Name: _____

IT'S ALL IN THE PAST featuring Al E. Gator and Jackrabbit Jim

Use the "It's All in the Past" maps to answer the following questions.

1. Between 1713 and 1763, which country lost most of its land?

_____

2. In 1763, as a result of the French and Indian War, France gave its land west of the Mississippi River to this country.

_____

3. In 1783, Spain owned the land that now makes up this southeastern state.

_____

4. Which part of mainland North America was not claimed by any of the countries listed in the map key?

_____

5. Between 1763 and 1783, this country lost most of its land in the east.

6. Between 1763 and 1783, what happened to much of the land owned by Britain?

_____

7. What event caused a major change in land ownership between 1763 and 1783?

_____

8. In 1783, what body of water marked the dividing line between Spanish and independent land?

_____

9. Based on the three maps, when did France own the most land?

_____

WRAP IT UP! Write two paragraphs explaining why changes in land ownership took place in America from 1713 to 1763 and again from 1763 to 1783.

IT'S ALL IN THE PAST: Historical Maps of North America

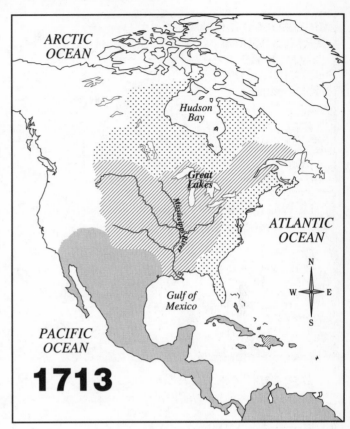

KEY

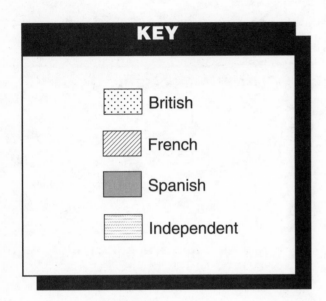

- :::: British
- //// French
- ▓▓ Spanish
- ≈≈ Independent

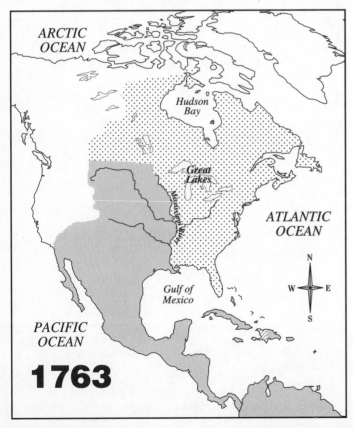

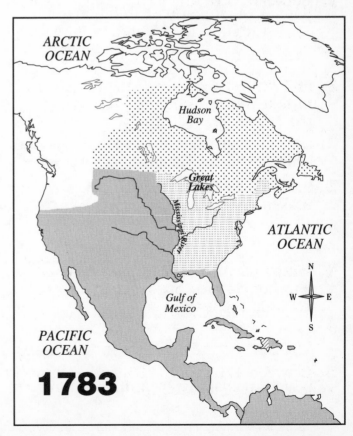

Name: _____

THE ART LESSON featuring Monkey Mike and Cowbella

Use "The Art Lesson" map to answer the following questions.

1. Name two temporary exhibitions that are featured at the Meadowpolitan.

_____

_____

2. If you just arrived at the Meadowpolitan, what would be the quickest way to get to Cowbella's paintings?

_____

_____

3. What type of decorative arts does the mooseum feature? In which room?

_____

4. Which rooms have paintings of animals?

5. What type of art is found in the majority of rooms at the mooseum?

_____

6. What type of architectural structures are exhibited at the Meadowpolitan?

_____

7. What can you find in the space below Room 20?

_____

8. How many restrooms are in the mooseum?

_____

WRAP IT UP! Draw a floorplan of your school and write questions for your classmates to answer.

Name: _____

THE ART LESSON: Map of the Meadowpolitan Mooseum of Art

GROUND FLOOR

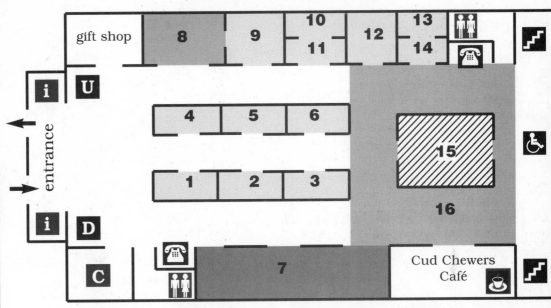

UPPER LEVEL

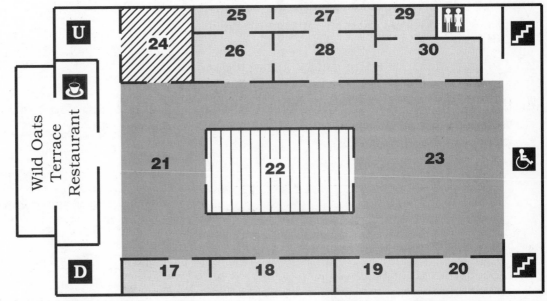

ACCESS

| U / D | escalator U = up D = down |

 staircase

 elevator for handicapped

SERVICES

restrooms

C cloakroom

telephone

restaurant services

i information

DEPARTMENTS

 **Painting**

Sculpture

Decorative Arts

Temporary Exhibitions

Architecture

Ground Floor Key:

1 Early American
2 Early American
3 Early American
4 20th Century
5 20th Century
6 20th Century
7 Weather vanes
8 Horses
9 Landscapes
10 Farmscapes
11 Farmscapes
12 Barns and silos
13 Pastures
14 Meadows
15 Farm photography
16 Marble sculptures

Upper Level Key:

17 1750–1800
18 1800–1850
19 1850–1900
20 1900–1950
21 Farm animals
22 Gazebos
23 Bovine beauties
24 Cowbella's paintings
25 Horses
26 Oxen
27 Pigs
28 Chickens
29 Still life
30 21st Century

ALL TURNED AROUND: page 5

1. East
2. North
3. West
4. South
5. East
6. North
7. North
8. West

Wrap It Up! The sun rises in the east and sets in the west. Once you know this you could figure out which way is north.

WHERE THERE'S SMOKE: page 6

1. Southwest
2. Northwest
3. Northeast
4. Northwest
5. Northeast
6. Southeast
7. Southwest
8. Southwest

Wrap It Up! Cardinal directions

FOOD FOR THOUGHT: page 7

1. The Piney Woods. See the image above right.
2. The cornfield. See the image above right.
3. Northwest
4. See the image above right. Her path was in the shape of a heart.
5. Four

Wrap It Up! Answers will vary.

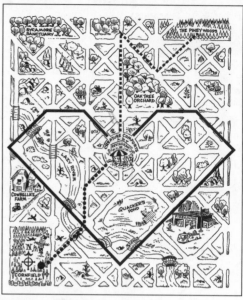

WRONG SIDE: page 9

1. See the image below.
2. West-northwest
3. East-southeast
4. East-northeast
5. South-southeast
6. See the image below.
7. North-northwest

Wrap It Up! Answers will vary.

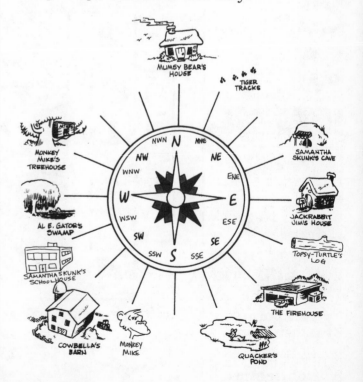

ANSWERS

IF AT FIRST: page 11
1. See the image below.
2. A heart. See the image below.
3. A star. See the image below.
4. A house. See the image below.

Wrap It Up! Answers will vary.

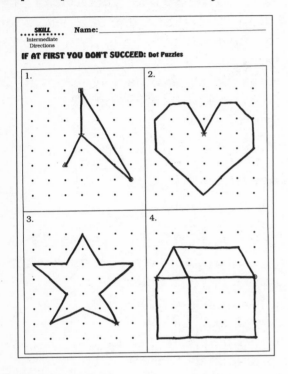

FLYING THE COOP: page 13
1. 45 degrees
2. 180 degrees
3. 180 degrees
4. 225 degrees
5. 90 degrees
6. 132 degrees
7. 323 degrees

Wrap It Up! North-northeast is 22.5 degrees, and west-southwest is 247.5 degrees.

LIVE AND LEARN: page 14
1. Check the cardinal and intermediate directions that the students added to their bearing boards.
2. 15 degrees
3. 120 degrees

4. 192.5 degrees
5. 257.5 degrees
6. 105 degrees
7. Check the students' bearing boards.
8. 135 degrees
9. 165 degrees

Wrap It Up! Sextants were navigational instruments used by early explorers to measure the angle between the horizon and a star to determine latitude.

MONKEY BUSINESS: page 16
1. A pond
2. Check the students' work. The pond on the map should be colored blue.
3. Woods
4. Check the students' work. The woods on the map should be colored green.
5. Fields
6. Check the students' work for accuracy.
7. See the image below.
8. See the image below.
9. See the image below.

Wrap It Up! Answers will vary

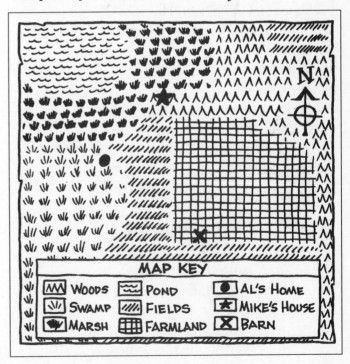

ANSWERS

CLASS ACT: page 17

1. See the image below.
2. See the image below.
3. Mt. Chamberlin
4. See the image below.
5. Point Barrow and Mendenhall Glacier
6. See the image below.
7. See the image below.
8. Mt. McKinley is 20,320 feet high.
9. North-northeast
10. See the image below.

Wrap It Up! Answers will vary.

OUT OF SIGHT: page 19

1. 3 miles
2. 2 miles
3. 6 miles
4. 1/2 mile
5. 1 mile farther
6. 8 miles
7. 22 miles

Wrap It Up! Northwest; southwest

MOVING DAY: page 20

(Accept a reasonable range of answers for these questions.)

1. Approximately 670 miles
2. Approximately 1,335 miles
3. Approximately 2,500 miles
4. Approximately 1,170 miles
5. Approximately 1,000 miles
6. Approximately 6,675 miles
7. Approximately 830 miles

Wrap It Up! The road distance would be longer because the roads do not go in a straight line from one city to another.

X MARKS THE SPOT: page 22

(Accept a reasonable range of answers for the measurement questions.)

1. Approximately 200 paces
2. Approximately 425 paces (Accept answers between 425 and 475.)
3. Tarantula Rock
4. 325 paces
5. 275 paces
6. Gator Bait Swamp
7. Vampire Bat Cave

BIRDS OF A FEATHER: page 24

(Accept a reasonable range of answers.)

1. Approximately 7 miles
2. Approximately 6 1/2 miles
3. Approximately 9 miles
4. Approximately 16 1/2 miles
5. Approximately 3 miles
6. 2 1/2 miles

Wrap It Up! Answers will vary.

MEASURE FOR MEASURE: page 25

(Accept a reasonable range of answers for these questions.)

1. Approximately 1,500 feet
2. Approximately 2,450 feet
3. Approximately 2,200 feet
4. Approximately 1,400 feet
5. Approximately 1,200 feet
6. Approximately 1,850 feet
7. Approximately 1,400 feet

PUZZLED: page 27

1. E7
2. C2, D2, E2, E3, E4, E5, E6
3. G3, G4, G5

4. B4
5. Northeast
6. East
7. Check the students' work for accuracy.
Wrap It Up! Answers will vary.

SCHOOL DAZE: page 28

1. C8
2. Answers will vary depending on the state in which you live.
3. D3
4. Oregon, Idaho, Montana, Nevada, Utah, and Wyoming
5. South Dakota: C3, C4, C5
   Iowa: C5, D5
   Missouri: D5, D6, E5, E6
   Kansas: D4, D5
   Colorado: D3, D4
   Wyoming: C2, C3, D2, D3
Wrap It Up! Answers will vary.

GO CLIMB A TREE: page 30

1. About 24°N
2. Gabon, Congo, Democratic Republic of Congo, Uganda, Kenya, and Ethiopia
3. The Tropic of Cancer
4. The Kalahari Desert
5. (Accept a reasonable range of answers.)
   Cape Town: 34°S
   Cairo: 30°N
   Nairobi: 2°S
   Khartoum: 16°N
6. Tripoli
Wrap It Up! Answers will vary depending on the state in which you live.

THE SPELLING BEE: page 32

1. Eastern
2. Western
3. 1°W
4. Norway, Russia, Finland, Belarus, Ukraine, and Turkey
5. 10°

6. 20°E and 30°E
7. Italy: 10°E
   Iceland: 20°W
   Sweden: 20°E
Wrap It Up! Answers will vary depending on the state in which you live.

THE DREAM TEAM: page 34

1. Approximately 33° 50'N; 117° 55'W
2. 42°N
3. Utah
4. Lake Tahoe
5. 119° 30'W
6. Santa Rosa Island
7. Approximately 40° 30'N; 121° 30'W
8. The Colorado River
Wrap It Up! Answers will vary depending on the city in which you live.

IN THE DOGHOUSE: page 36

1. 1:00 P.M.
2. East
3. Mountain
4. Five hours
5. 180°
6. Pacific
7. Anchorage: 10:00 P.M.
   Chicago: 1:00 A.M.
   Washington, D.C.: 2:00 A.M.
   Helena: 12:00 A.M.
Wrap It Up! Suggested answers: If you want to do business with someone in another state, you need to call during business hours. You wouldn't want to call someone in the middle of the night.

THE NAME GAME: page 38

1. Delaware, Pennsylvania, and New York
2. Delaware River, Delaware Bay, Atlantic Ocean, Lower Bay, and Hudson River
3. New York
4. Delaware River

Answers

5. Trenton, NJ, and Dover, DE
6. Cumberland County, Atlantic County, Delaware Bay, and Atlantic Ocean
7. None

Wrap It Up! There is usually a sign telling you when you're entering a different state. There might be a Welcome Center.

QUEEN OF THE NILE: page 40
1. The White Nile and the Blue Nile
2. Khartoum, Sudan
3. Red Sea and Mediterranean Sea
4. Israel, Libya, and Sudan
5. Seven
6. Lake Malawi, Lake Tanganyika, and the Indian Ocean
7. Lesotho
8. Niger, Chad, Cameroon, and Nigeria
9. Madagascar

Wrap It Up! Answers will vary depending on the state in which you live.

THE ROAD TRIP: page 42
1. Interstate 17
2. North and south
3. Southwest
4. Interstate 8 and Interstate 10
5. Gallup, NM
6. State highway
7. Kingman, AZ; Flagstaff, AZ; Holbrook, AZ; and Gallup, NM
8. The Grand Canyon

Wrap It Up! Check students' maps for accuracy.

GO FIGURE: page 44
1. Lower
2. The Allegheny Mountains
3. Mount Davis is 3,213 feet high
4. Philadelphia
5. 1,800–3,000 feet
6. Below sea level
7. Southwest

8. Uphill
9. The Delaware River and Lake Erie

Wrap It Up! Answers will vary depending on the state in which you live.

THE DOCTOR IS IN: page 46
1. 50 to 100 people per square mile
2. Germany
3. Northern Europe
4. 20 to 40 people per square kilometer
5. 0 to 5 people per square mile
6. Increase
7. Athens, Bucharest, Moscow
8. The Arctic Circle

Wrap It Up! Answers will vary.

DOLLARS AND SENSE: page 48
1. Corn
2. Petroleum and silver
3. Gold and silver
4. Eastern Montana
5. Coal, gold, silver, petroleum, natural gas
6. Cattle and poultry
7. Corn, vegetables, and wheat
8. Southwest Montana
9. Petroleum

Wrap It Up! Answers will vary.

FAIR-WEATHER FRIENDS: page 50
1. Miami
2. Portland
3. Jackson Hole
4. Eight
5. Stationary front
6. Denver
7. Zero
8. Summer

Wrap It Up! Answers will vary depending on the state in which you live.

ANSWERS

TAKE A HIKE: page 52

1. 6.75 miles
2. .5 miles
3. 2.25 miles
4. .25 miles
5. Wriggle
6. 5.5 miles
7. Echo Canyon would have a better sunset because it faces west.

Wrap It Up! Answers will vary.

IT'S ALL IN THE PAST: page 54

1. France
2. Spain
3. Florida
4. Northwest
5. Great Britain
6. It became independent.
7. The Revolutionary War
8. The Mississippi River
9. 1713

Wrap It Up! In short, the French and Indian War caused the major changes between 1713 and 1763, while the Revolutionary War brought about the major changes between 1763 and 1783.

THE ART LESSON: page 56

1. Farm photography and Cowbella's paintings
2. Go up the escalator by the gift shop and proceed to Room 24.
3. Weather vanes are in Room 7.
4. Rooms 25, 26, 27, and 28
5. Painting
6. Gazebos
7. The Cud Chewers Café
8. Three

Wrap It Up! Answers will vary.

NOTES